UNDER YOUR FEET

Written by **Dr. Jackie Stroud**

RHS Author and Consultant **Dr. Marc Redmile-Gordon**

Illustrated by **Wenjia Tang**

CONTENTS

DK | Penguin Random House

Written by Dr Jackie Stroud, Dr Marc Redmile-Gordon
Illustrated by Wenjia Tang

Editor Kathleen Teece
Senior Commissioning Designer Fiona Macdonald
Design Assistant Katherine Marriott
US Senior Editor Shannon Beatty
US Editor Jane Perlmutter
Managing Editors Laura Gilbert, Jonathan Melmoth
Managing Art Editor Diane Peyton Jones
Project Art Editor Jaileen Kaur
Senior Picture Researcher Sumedha Chopra
Senior Pre-Producer Nikoleta Parasaki
Producer Ena Matagic
Senior DTP Designer Jagtar Singh
Creative Directors Helen Senior, Clare Baggaley
Publishing Director Sarah Larter
RHS Publisher Rae Spencer-Jones
RHS Editors Simon Maughan, Guy Barter
RHS Head of Editorial Chris Young

First American Edition, 2020
Published in the United States by DK Publishing
1745 Broadway, 20th Floor, New York, NY 10019

Copyright © 2020 Dorling Kindersley Limited
DK, a Division of Penguin Random House LLC
23 24 25 26   10 9 8 7 6 5 4 3
009–316657–Apr/2020

A catalog record for this book
is available from the Library of Congress.
ISBN 978-1-4654-9095-7

DK books are available at special discounts when purchased in bulk
for sales promotions, premiums, fund-raising, or educational use.
For details, contact: DK Publishing Special Markets,
1745 Broadway, 20th Floor, New York, NY 10019
SpecialSales@dk.com

Printed and bound in China

For the curious
www.dk.com

MIX
Paper | Supporting
responsible forestry
FSC™ C018179

This book was made with Forest
Stewardship Council™ certified paper—
one small step in DK's commitment to a
sustainable future. For more information
go to www.dk.com/our-green-pledge

WHY DO WE NEED SOIL?

We often brush soil off newly bought mushrooms and vegetables. These are some of the foods that use the nutrients and water stored in soil to grow. Soil has a lot of other important jobs, too, from holding up houses to cleaning water.

Without soil to absorb it, rain can cause floods.

Soil absorbs rain.

Animals release CO_2.

Filtering water

Soil is the largest water filter on Earth. As water flows downward through the soil, small pores (openings) trap murky bits in the water. Soil also absorbs some harmful substances that have made it into the water.

Getting rid of waste

Living things in soil eat organic waste and release it as nutrients into the soil, which help plants grow.

Saving the planet

A gas called carbon dioxide (CO_2) traps heat in the air and makes our planet warmer. Soil stores carbon (found in CO_2), so protecting it could help slow global warming.

Foundations

Cracks can appear if part of the house starts to sink.

Houses are built on foundations that are dug into the soil. If the soil becomes unstable then foundations can slip and the house may start to sink.

Food

Many animals need soil-growing plants to eat. Other animals, in turn, need to eat those animals to survive.

Green spaces

Green spaces are full of plants that absorb CO_2 and release oxygen. Soil creates a sturdy foundation for roots. It provides a reserve of nutrients and water that plants use to grow.

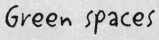

Capture carbon

Carbon is found as a solid and in CO_2. Solid carbon is found in trees, and is released into the soil when they rot. It can more easily become CO_2 from the soil. Making some trees into furniture can actually lock the carbon up longer!

Tread lightly

We create greenhouse gases by driving or walking on wet soil. Air is squashed out of the soil, which leads to more nitrous oxide and methane in the air.

Grow things

Plants change CO_2 into solid carbon, such as sugars, to make their leaves and roots. When they die, the carbon becomes part of the soil.

Plants feed soil microbes with carbon from their roots.

The atmosphere is a layer of gases around the Earth.

GLOBAL WARMING

Soil helps keep our planet at the right temperature—not too hot or cold. Soil can produce greenhouse gases that make climate change worse. We can help soil soak up these gases, however, by taking care of the ground.

Make airy compost

A lot of nitrous oxide and methane is made by microorganisms that do not have enough oxygen (a gas found in the air). Compost piles need a lot of dry leaves, twigs, and other materials that let air in for the microorganisms to breathe.

Farm wisely

Farmers plow soil to kill weeds. Plowing also breaks the soil up, which releases nutrients to help seeds grow. Too much plowing, however, destroys soil life and releases greenhouse gases. Many farmers are choosing to plow less to help solve this problem.

It is warmed by the sun's rays.

Greenhouse gases

The Earth is heating up, which causes fires, droughts, and floods. We call this global warming. The three main "greenhouse" gases that cause it are carbon dioxide (CO_2), nitrous oxide (N_2O), and methane (CH_4).

Carbon dioxide

Nitrous oxide

Methane

THE STUFF OF SOIL

Soil is like a cake mix—made up of ingredients. The four ingredients in soil are minerals, water, air, and organic matter (living or once-living things). Different combinations of each make up different types of soil.

Soil can fill up with water so it pools on the surface.

Water

Water soaks into the soil after it rains. Minerals and nutrients dissolve into the water to form a soil solution. Most water drains through burrows and cracks, but some will remain in small spaces between soil particles, called pores.

20-30%

Organic matter

Living roots and millions of soil organisms, from microscopic fungi to creepy-crawly bugs, are all organic matter. This also includes dead things, such as leaves that are decaying (breaking down).

Larvae

Decayed leaves

5%

Beetles lay eggs in soil, which hatch into larvae.

Leaves take 6 to 12 months to decompose.

Broccoli grows well in clay soil, which stores a lot of water and nutrients.

In overly wet soil, water fills airy spaces.

Air

Organisms live and grow best in soil with almost equal amounts of air and water, which they need to survive. Air moves through the soil in cracks, burrows, and pores.

Centipedes absorb air through holes along their bodies.

20-30%

Beetles begin their lives underground, where they need air to breathe.

Bedrock

45%

Clay

Sand

Silt

Turnips grow well in loose, sandy soil.

Minerals

A mineral is a solid that is found naturally and made of crystals. In soil, the gritty mineral ingredient includes particles called sand, silt, and clay. Some plants grow well in sandy soil, but others prefer soil with a lot of clay particles.

Sand particles can be 1,000 times bigger than clay.

Soil minerals are worn away from rocks on the surface and from bedrock.

SOIL HORIZONS

Our lifetimes are short compared to the thousands of years it can take for soil to form into layers, called horizons. Soil can stretch down for 164 ft (50 m).

Millipedes and other soil dwellers eat humus for its nutrients.

Humus

The top portion of soil is called humus. This dark horizon is made of dead things that have decayed (broken down).

Topsoil

You might have seen the mid-brown topsoil layer if you've planted seeds near the surface of soil. This mixture of dead matter, minerals, and small rock fragments is where most soil animals live.

Subsoil

A lot of digging would reveal this pale layer. Among tree roots, there are minerals and materials carried down by rainwater from above.

Mineral spotting

Cassiterite

Schorl

Beryl

Turquoise

Pyrite

Howlite

Regolith

Digging starts to get difficult in the deep, substratum layer. This horizon is full of minerals and large rock fragments. Pieces of these become the material in the upper layers.

Bedrock

Anyone tunneling down into the soil would eventually hit this solid slab of rock with a bang. Bedrock has not been broken down by wind or rain, unlike surface rock.

Hematite

Sodalite

Small creatures can leave their outlines in bedrock.

Bedrock is not soil, and always sits beneath the horizons.

SOIL CITY

About a third of all creatures on the planet live in soil. Most rely on their fellow soil dwellers for food. Some poop out nutrients for plants to eat. Scientists often group the animals together by size.

Slugs

Hyphae are the skinny parts of fungi that absorb soil nutrients.

Plant root

Fungi and plants

Fungi release chemicals, called enzymes, which break down dead plants into nutrients. The fungi, as well as plants, can then absorb these nutrients to grow.

Springtails can spring (jump) as high as a pencil.

Earthworms

These wigglers eat dead plants and make poop containing a lot of nutrients. Soil organisms eat the poop to get the nutrients.

Mites are the fastest-running land animal for their size.

Moles burrow to 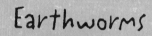 catch unsuspecting worms.

Moles

You may never see a worm-guzzling mole because it spends most of its life below ground. However, piles of freshly dug soil are a sign of moles beneath.

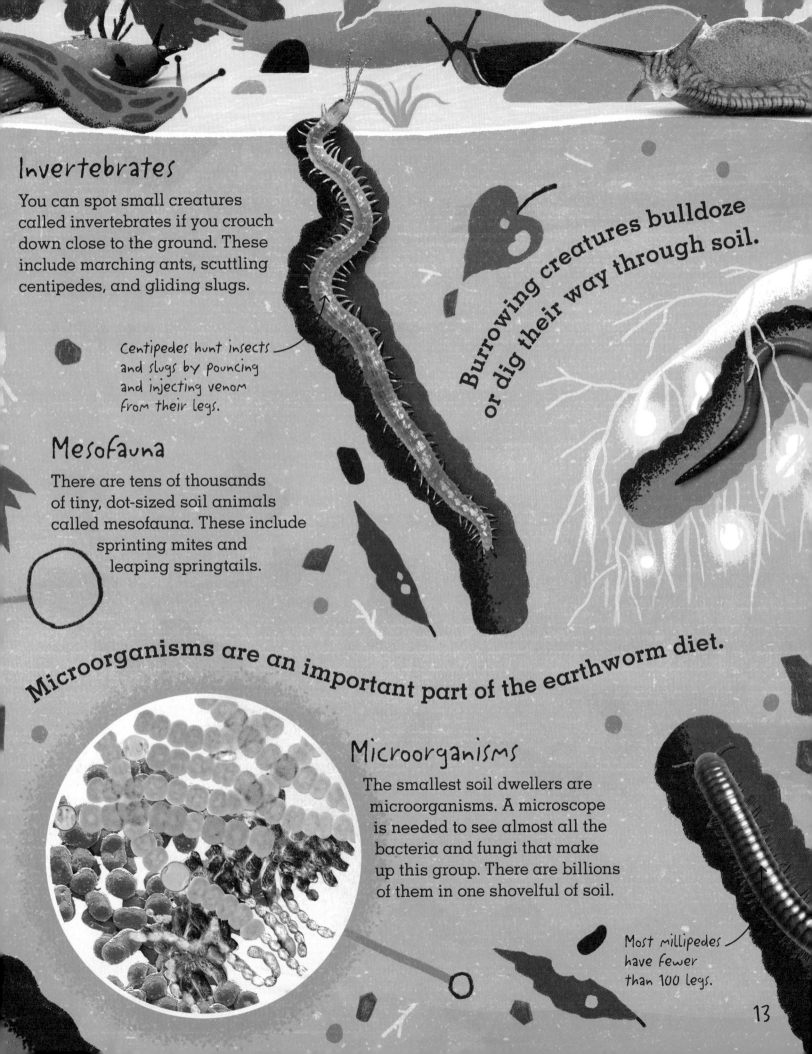

Invertebrates

You can spot small creatures called invertebrates if you crouch down close to the ground. These include marching ants, scuttling centipedes, and gliding slugs.

Centipedes hunt insects and slugs by pouncing and injecting venom from their legs.

Mesofauna

There are tens of thousands of tiny, dot-sized soil animals called mesofauna. These include sprinting mites and leaping springtails.

Burrowing creatures bulldoze or dig their way through soil.

Microorganisms are an important part of the earthworm diet.

Microorganisms

The smallest soil dwellers are microorganisms. A microscope is needed to see almost all the bacteria and fungi that make up this group. There are billions of them in one shovelful of soil.

Most millipedes have fewer than 100 legs.

LEEK

ONION

Leeks are able
to last through
snowy weather.

Fibrous roots

These roots
grow downward and
outward from the main
stem of the plant.

The white part
of a leek is
formed from
the bases of
its leaves.

Bulbs

A bulb is a stem, which
holds up the parts of the
plant above. It stores
water and transports it
from the roots beneath
to the leaves above.

The bulb
grows in
spherical
layers.

Fibrous roots
grow out of
the bulb in a
tangled bunch.

SHOOTS AND ROOTS

You only need to look at a chunky
carrot and the thin tendrils sprouting from
leeks to know that roots come in different
shapes and sizes. Noodlelike fibrous roots
and thick taproots spread out in the soil
beneath vegetable gardens.

BEET

CARROT

The leaves grow above ground.

The round part of a beet is its stem.

Roots can be cone-shaped.

Sugar is stored in a carrot's taproot. The sugar gives the plant energy to grow.

Bright beets take around 120 days to grow.

More roots grow sideways from the main taproot.

Taproots

Carrots and other taproots take up much more space than spindly fibrous roots. They grow downward from the middle of the plant, burrowing deep into the soil to find water.

Taproots grow deep down into the ground.

15

GROWING FOOD

The fruits, vegetables, beans, and grains that fill our plates all need healthy soil to grow. Farmers take great care of the soil used for their crops.

Slugs and other pests eat crops and earthworms.

In healthy soil, there are creatures such as beetles to eat pests such as slugs.

Sowing seeds

Seeds are planted at an exact depth. Too shallow, and birds will gobble them up. Too deep, and the seedlings won't grow!

Health check

Good soil feels crumbly and has plenty of earthworms in it. Farmers dig holes to check that their soil is healthy for growing crops.

Scarecrows can scare off birds that have their greedy eyes on the seeds.

Corn can be ground into flour and used to make tortillas.

China produces the most wheat in the world.

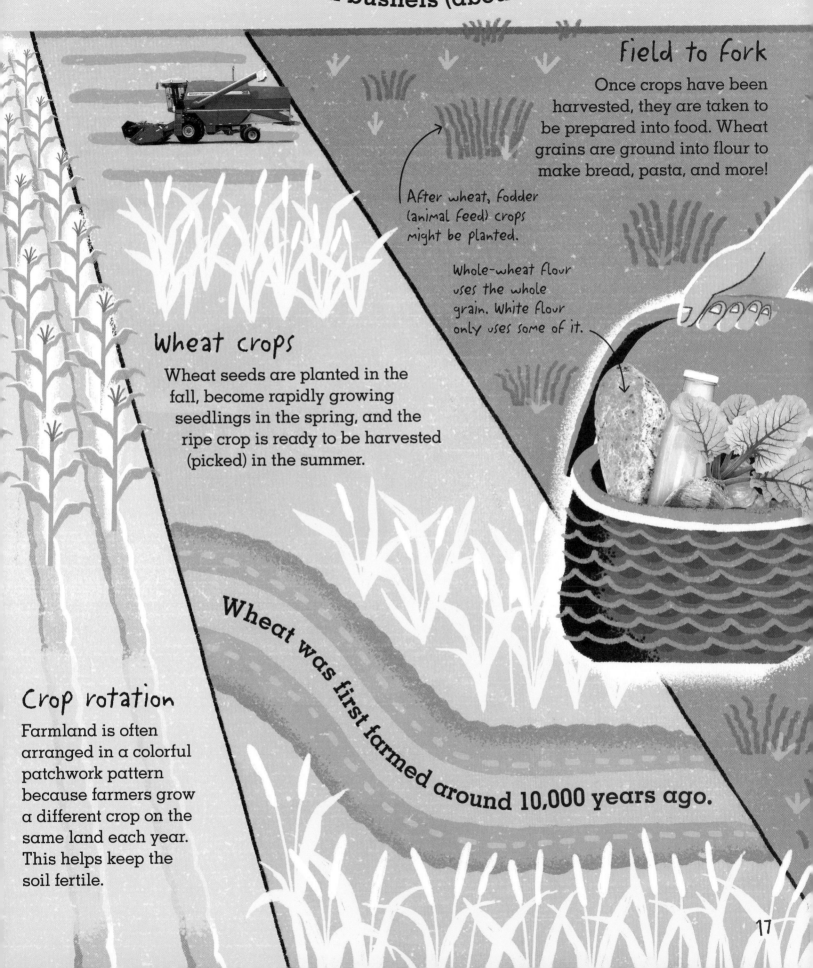

Field to fork

Once crops have been harvested, they are taken to be prepared into food. Wheat grains are ground into flour to make bread, pasta, and more!

After wheat, fodder (animal feed) crops might be planted.

Whole-wheat flour uses the whole grain. White flour only uses some of it.

Wheat crops

Wheat seeds are planted in the fall, become rapidly growing seedlings in the spring, and the ripe crop is ready to be harvested (picked) in the summer.

Wheat was first farmed around 10,000 years ago.

Crop rotation

Farmland is often arranged in a colorful patchwork pattern because farmers grow a different crop on the same land each year. This helps keep the soil fertile.

Birds catch worms to feed to their chicks.

A WORM'S WORK

Earthworms do a lot of hidden jobs, especially in the spring and the fall. This is when most soil is warm and moist. The three main types of earthworm are surface worms, topsoil worms, and deep burrowers.

Wildlife Food

Earthworms are an important food for wildlife such as birds and foxes. Foxes catch up to 10 juicy worms a minute.

Different types of earthworms live at different depths.

Leaf decomposers

Red surface worms usually grow to the size of a matchstick. These worms feed on dead leaves near the soil surface. They poop the nutrients from the leaves into the soil.

Surface worms live on top of the soil.

Off-duty worms

Soil can become too dry for earthworms. Then, the worms make small chambers, and curl up into tight knots to rest and avoid losing moisture. This can be for days or months, until the soil conditions improve.

Mucus-lined chambers help worms survive the summer.

Plant chefs

Pale topsoil worms eat soil, and poop it out in a different form. Plants absorb this as food. Topsoil worms can be more than three times as long as surface worms.

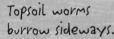
Topsoil worms burrow sideways.

Worms of the deep

Deep burrowing worms are about the size of a pen. They are powerful burrowers, who make and maintain vertical burrows.

Deep burrowers live for up to 10 years.

Adults have a saddle (ring) near their head.

Casts (poops) fill up the burrows, so the worms make new ones.

Casts provide much-needed nutrients for plant roots.

Young earthworms have smooth bodies.

Plant Food

Plants can't just absorb other plant matter as food. They need it to be broken down into nutrient-rich material by worms or microorganisms.

Worm plumbers

Undisturbed vertical burrows can last for 30 years. These are important channels, which allow water and air to move through the soil.

19

1 From tree to ground

In the fall, many leaves burst into red, orange, and yellow colors. This means they're almost ready to drop from trees and shrubs. Soon, they will die and fall to the ground.

Trees that lose their leaves yearly are called deciduous.

2 Broken up

At night, soil animals, such as millipedes and earthworms, shred the dead leaves into small pieces to eat. This also makes the leaves easier to eat for other soil dwellers.

Millipedes eat plant material such as dead leaves.

3 Down into the soil

Earthworms gather the leaves and bits of leaves into piles, called middens, on the soil surface. Bit by bit, the middens are dragged into the burrows.

DECOMPOSING

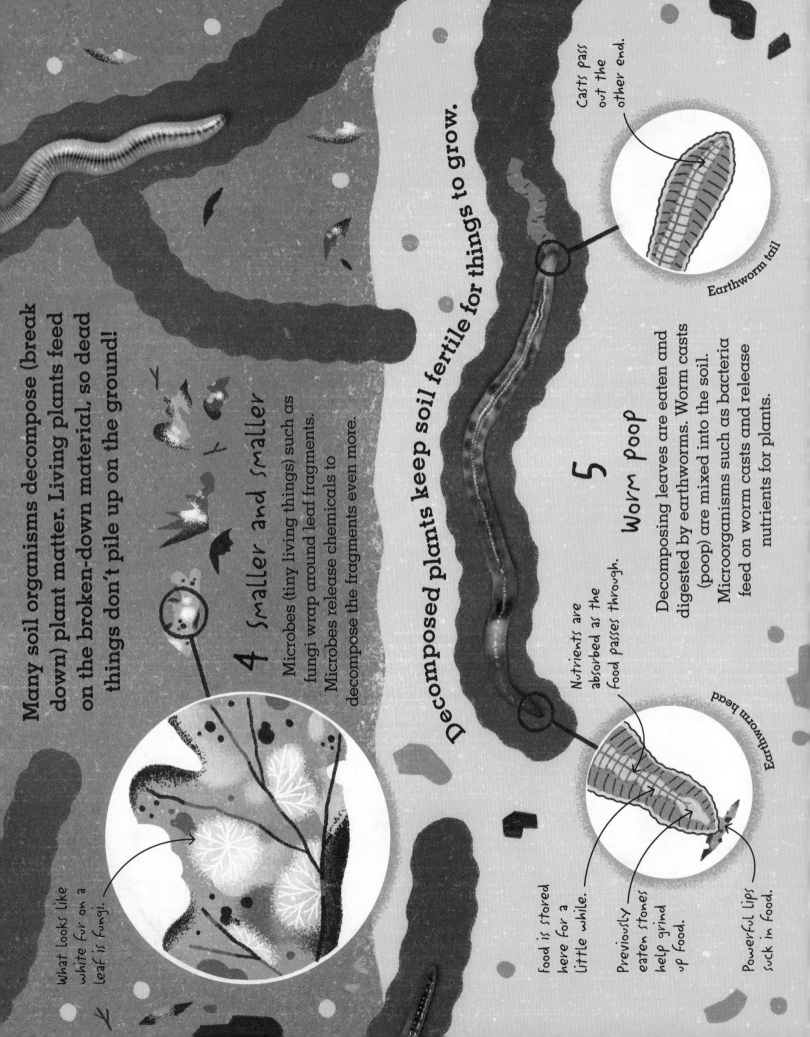

Many soil organisms decompose (break down) plant matter. Living plants feed on the broken-down material, so dead things don't pile up on the ground!

What looks like white fur on a leaf is fungi.

4 Smaller and smaller

Microbes (tiny living things) such as fungi wrap around leaf fragments. Microbes release chemicals to decompose the fragments even more.

Decomposed plants keep soil fertile for things to grow.

Casts pass out the other end.

Earthworm tail

5 Worm poop

Decomposing leaves are eaten and digested by earthworms. Worm casts (poop) are mixed into the soil. Microorganisms such as bacteria feed on worm casts and release nutrients for plants.

Nutrients are absorbed as the food passes through.

Earthworm head

Food is stored here for a little while.

Previously eaten stones help grind up food.

Powerful lips suck in food.

DRY SOIL

Dry desert soil is home to plants that can live without rain for long periods of time. Plants are few and far between, but they have amazing abilities to absorb water.

Prickles protect the stem from thirsty creatures.

A chunky stem stores water for the plant to use.

Cactus

A network of shallow, wide-spreading roots helps the plant drink as much water as possible if it rains.

Thick, spongy bark holds water.

A pebbly disguise keeps plant-eating animals away.

The roots can go far to find water.

Living stones

Pebble plants can absorb water from fog. During droughts they shrink below ground, so they need even less water.

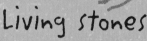

Some cacti can last for two years without rain.

Saxaul tree

This tree's root networks hold large amounts of dry sand in place. Planting more of them stops soil from blowing away.

SOGGY SOIL

Rain forests are home to thousands of plants, but the soil is shallow and poor. Up to 400 inches (10 m) of rain a year washes the nutrients away. Some smart plants live on each other, instead!

Rain forests get ten times as much rain as deserts.

Fig plants wrap around tree trunks.

Strangler Fig

This plant's seeds sprout in the moist, nutrient-rich treetops. The seedlings grow down to the forest floor and eventually take root in the soil.

Animals eat the figs, and their poop spreads the seeds.

Fungi on the roots help the plant absorb nutrients.

Buttress roots

Tall trees have thick buttress roots that grow out from the trunk above ground for stability. Nutrients are near the soil surface, so tree roots are shallow.

BEAUTIFUL BOGS

Squishy, muddy peat bogs are found in wetland areas. They are home to some unique and beautiful plants. The soil, called peat, can preserve ancient objects and bodies.

Deer grass

How is peat made?

Boggy ground has little oxygen. Most microbes need this to decompose dead things. Most bogs are also too acidic for these microbes to live in. So dead plants build up in layers to form peat.

Common frog

Barrels of butter up to 2,000 years old are some of the strangest bog finds.

Ancient things

Some things last for thousands of years in bogs without breaking down. The bodies of ancient people, called bog bodies, have even been found!

Azure hawker dragonfly

Cross-leaved heath

24

Global warming

Carbon dioxide (CO_2) is a gas that traps heat and makes the Earth warmer. Peat stores large amounts of carbon (found in CO_2), so protecting bogs could help to slow global warming.

Peat contains as much carbon as is found in the air.

Hen harrier

Plenty of plants

Peat bogs are habitats for rare plants such as sphagnum moss. These tiny plants look like a multicolored carpet because they grow so close together.

Hare's tail cotton grass

Peat is formed over many thousands of years.

Golden plover

In the past, many people dried and burned peat to heat cooking stoves.

Sphagnum moss

Emperor dragonfly

Black soil

Peat is mostly made up of partly decomposed plants. This makes it black in color. It feels soft and spongy to touch.

25

SUN, WIND, AND RAIN

Heavy rain might make us very wet, but it also washes away bare soil. Soil needs plants to protect it from all kinds of weather, from splashy rains to burning sunshine and howling winds!

Whirling columns of air and soil are called dust devils.

Baked dry

Dry soil is kept in place by plants. If bare soil is baked dry by the sun, wind can blow it away.

Plant leaves can protect the soil from raindrops.

Plant roots hold soil in place.

Splashed away

A drop of rain can be bad for soil. Raindrops hitting the ground with a lot of force dislodge soil particles and wash them away.

Muddy floods

Soil on hilly land without plant roots to anchor it in place is in danger. Too much rain causes floods that can wash the soil away.

Weathered downstream

Soil taken away by weather is washed into rivers and carried out to sea. The soil that took thousands of years to form is lost forever.

Snow can protect grass from freezing temperatures that might damage it.

It takes 500 years for 1 in (2.5 cm) of soil to form.

Frozen solid

Farmers might leave fields unplanted over winter so that crop diseases go away. Cold weather can freeze bare soil in place to stop it from being carried away by wind.

27

AWAKE AT NIGHT

The ground is alive with activity at night. Nocturnal animals sleep all day and awaken when you're in bed. They scurry around to find food in the moonlight.

Some animals can see in the dark.

Furtive foragers

Small creatures often forage (search) for food, such as berries, at night. It is safer in the dark because it's harder for predators to see them.

Mice forage for meals of nuts and fruit.

Antlion larvae (young) dig pits that trap ants to eat.

Ground hunters

Ground hunters rest during the day in damp, dark places such as underneath rocks. They emerge at night to hunt nocturnal foragers.

Giant centipedes are deadly insect hunters.

Beetles hunt juicy caterpillars and grubs.

Flying fiends

Many nocturnal birds are fierce hunters that swoop down to catch prey on the ground. The Australian owlet-nightjar catches crickets and ants that emerge after sunset.

Singing insects

High-pitched chirping sounds can fill the night. Insects such as crickets make the noise by rubbing body parts together, often to attract females.

Bull ants forage for food between dusk and dawn.

Night-blooming flowers

Some cacti only bloom at night. The flowers attract winged creatures that carry pollen to other flowers, which need the pollen to make seeds.

FUNGUS KINGDOM

A poisonous toadstool in the forest is just one part of a fungus—as is a mushroom in your kitchen fridge! Fungi can be vast soil organisms or tiny microbes, without which many plants couldn't grow.

Violet webcap

What are fungi?

Fungi are not plants, animals, or bacteria. They have a stringy body made up of thousands of tiny threads that spread throughout the soil.

Fly agaric

Gliophorus viridis

Orange peel

Plant pals

Fungi can live on plant roots. They take nutrients from the soil for the plant and receive food in return.

Fungal food

Fungi have no mouths or stomachs. They absorb their food directly, or release chemicals called enzymes that break it down so it can be absorbed.

Spores are like miniscule seeds.

Werewere-kokako

This fungus is named after the kokako bird's blue wattle.

Oyster mushroom

Mushrooms can be edible, but many are poisonous!

Field mushroom

Velvet foot

Magical mushrooms

A mushroom is the part of a fungus that grows out of the soil to release spores. Wind carries the spores away, which grow into new mushrooms.

Hen of the woods

Fungi don't have leaves, roots, or stems.

Star mushrooms erupt a smokelike cloud of spores.

Humongous fungus

The largest organism on Earth is a fungus. It spreads out for 3.4 sq miles (8.8 sq km) beneath an entire forest in Oregon, US.

Tiger worms have a striped body and no teeth. They have powerful lip muscles and suck food into their mouth.

Tiger Worms

Tiger worms are found in outside compost bins.

Tiger worms eat leaves and scraps of fruit and vegetables.

Mixing it up

Earthworms mix the different soil layers together. This spreads out organic (living or once-living) matter and releases nutrients for soil animals to eat.

WONDERFUL WORMS

They spend their lives hidden from sight, unless you know where to look. Lift the lid of a compost bin to find stripy tiger worms, dig a hole to see pink, green, and even yellow-tailed earthworms, and at the beach look out for wiggly piles of sand made by burrowing sandworms.

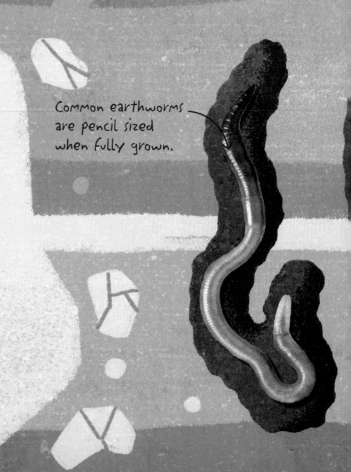

Common earthworms are pencil sized when fully grown.

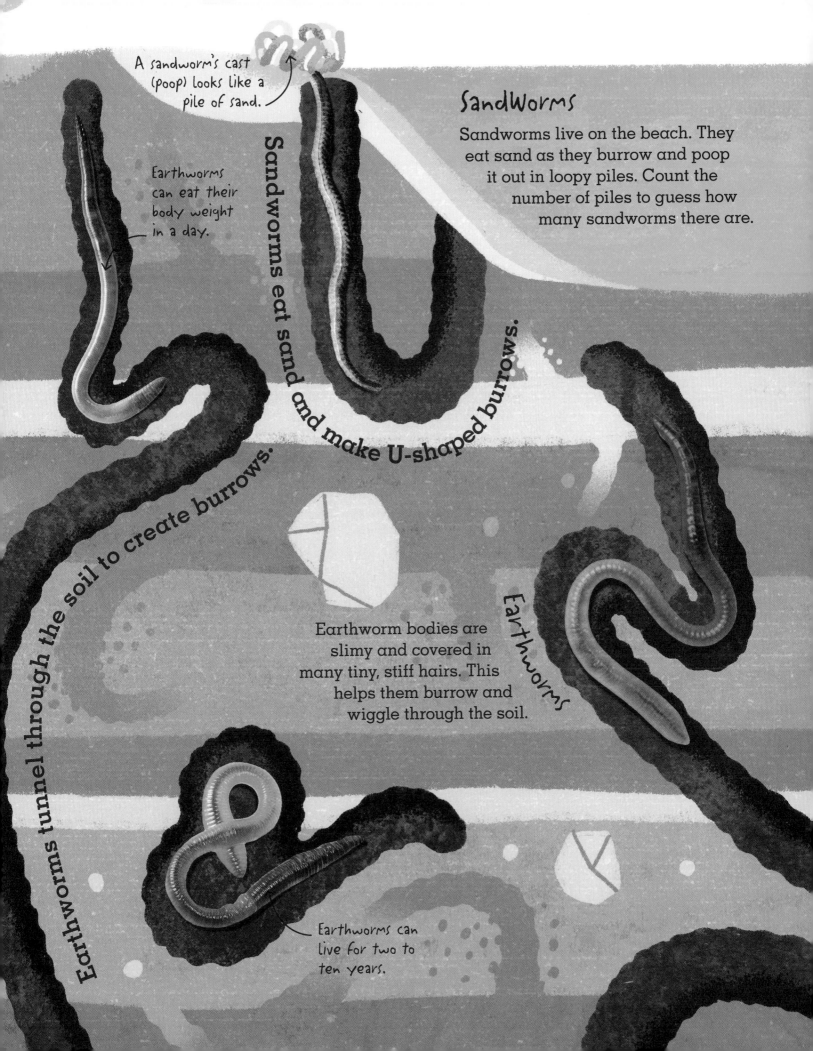

A sandworm's cast (poop) looks like a pile of sand.

Earthworms can eat their body weight in a day.

Sandworms eat sand and make U-shaped burrows.

SandWorms

Sandworms live on the beach. They eat sand as they burrow and poop it out in loopy piles. Count the number of piles to guess how many sandworms there are.

Earthworms tunnel through the soil to create burrows.

Earthworm bodies are slimy and covered in many tiny, stiff hairs. This helps them burrow and wiggle through the soil.

Earthworms

Earthworms can live for two to ten years.

Star-nosed mole

Tentacles around this mole's mouth can detect the electrical signals of nearby prey. The star-nosed mole is the fastest eating mammal on Earth!

MARVELOUS MOLES

Beneath your feet a mole could be prowling through its dark network of underground tunnels. It spends most of its time digging and waiting for wormy prey to fall through the soily ceiling.

Eastern mole

This mole lives in North America. Like most moles, it has spadelike hands to help dig through the soil.

Eastern moles are nearly blind— they have no need to see underground.

Molehill

The soil dug out by moles as they burrow gets tossed into piles, called molehills.

Long-tailed weasels eat moles and can invade their tunnels.

Tunnels might be used by multiple moles over time, if the mole moves out!

Feeding tunnel

Mole tunnels are deadly traps for worms. The burrowing worms fall through from the soil above. This causes vibrations (ground movement) that the mole quickly moves toward.

Baby moles are hairless until the age of about two weeks.

Moles live by themselves and fight off invaders.

Nest

This chamber is lined with soft piles of dried leaves and grass. Moles give birth and keeps their babies safe here.

Worm pantry

A toxin in mole spit can paralyze worms. This means they are alive, but can't move. "Pantries" are made to store hundreds of paralyzed worms.

Most moles are smaller than your foot!

BURROWERS

Have you ever seen a creature disappear into a hole? This could be the entrance to a network of tunnels and chambers, called burrows.

Striped-faced badgers eat rabbits.

Coyotes wait hungrily for gophers to pop up.

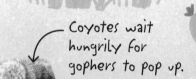

Gophers push soil up to the surface as they dig, which leaves long mounds on the surface.

Rabbit hole

European rabbits graze on plants above ground, at dusk and dawn. If a predator disturbs them, they dive into their tunnel network, which is called a warren.

Gopher town

American pocket gophers use their claws and huge teeth to dig tunnels. They pop out of holes to eat plants. Their burrows include deep nests and food-storage chambers.

Aardvarks may dig temporary burrows to hide from lions.

Aardvark park

African aardvarks live in their cool, underground burrows during the hot day. They forage at night for termites, using their long tongue to lap up insects.

Aardvarks destroy termite mounds to get to their prey.

Chipmunks dive into burrows before bobcats can eat them.

Most predators can't fit in burrows.

Chipmunk county

There's no mound of soil by the entrance of a chipmunk burrow because they carry away the dug-up soil in their cheeks. The burrows have many entrances and chambers of nuts and seeds.

37

Instead of pee, wood lice release a gas from their shells.

Wood lice like to nibble rotting wood and leaves.

Wood lice

Pill bug and sow bug are alternative names for wood lice. They are crustaceans, like shellfish.

Wood lice roll into a ball for protection from predators.

Insects

Insects have six legs and their bodies are divided into three parts. Many insects live underground. Bumblebees sleep in soil during winter.

Some cicadas spend their first 17 years below ground.

Prey step on the webbed tunnels of some spiders. The web vibrates so the spider knows they are there.

Spiders

Spiders have eight scuttling legs. They range from pinhead sized to ones that are bigger than your hand! Spiders make sticky webs to catch prey such as insects.

Slug

SPINELESS INVERTEBRATES

Animals without backbones make up 90 percent of all creatures on Earth. These are called invertebrates, and the ground is crawling with them.

Velvet worms shoot slime at prey that hardens to stop them from escaping.

Mollusks

Mollusks move around on a large, slimy foot. Most mollusks have shells. Snails have shells that they live in. They use their shell to hide from predators.

Snail

Velvet worms

The soft texture of these creepy-crawlies gives them their name. They look like worms but have a lot of legs.

Each leg has a tiny pair of claws.

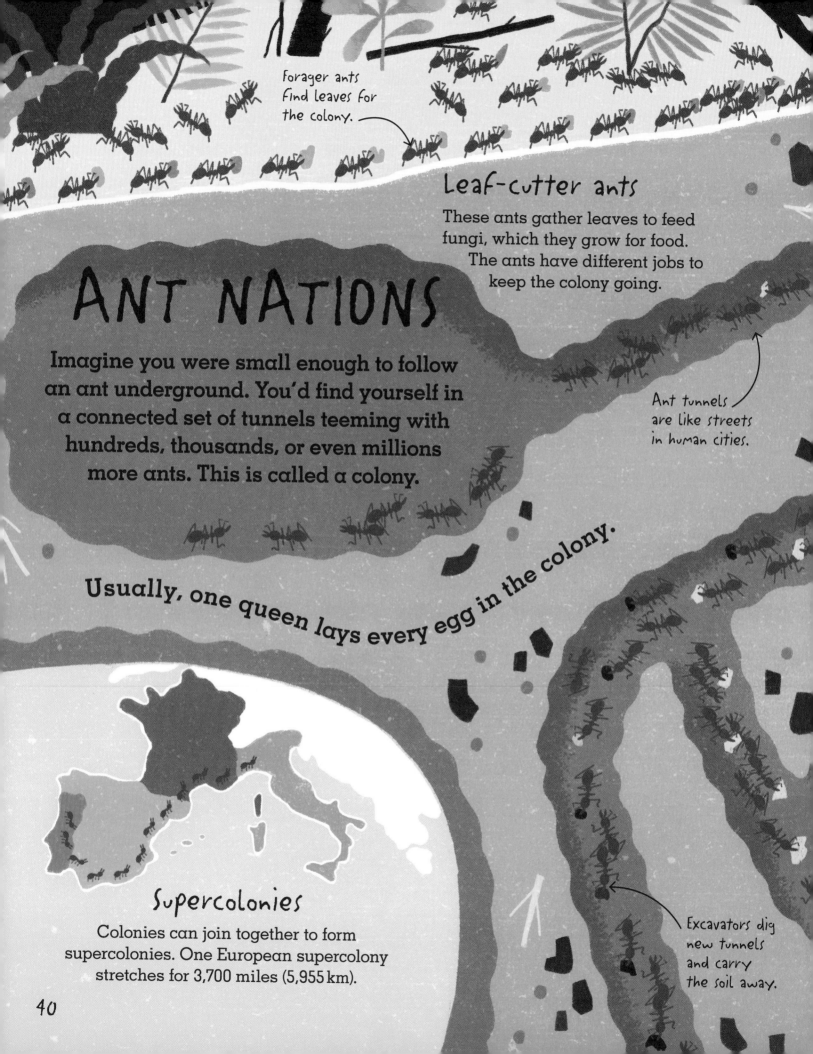

Forager ants find leaves for the colony.

Leaf-cutter ants

These ants gather leaves to feed fungi, which they grow for food. The ants have different jobs to keep the colony going.

ANT NATIONS

Imagine you were small enough to follow an ant underground. You'd find yourself in a connected set of tunnels teeming with hundreds, thousands, or even millions more ants. This is called a colony.

Ant tunnels are like streets in human cities.

Usually, one queen lays every egg in the colony.

Supercolonies

Colonies can join together to form supercolonies. One European supercolony stretches for 3,700 miles (5,955 km).

Excavators dig new tunnels and carry the soil away.

Soldier ants will bite attackers to defend the colony.

Phorid flies lay eggs inside some ants.

When finding leaves, a scent is left for others to follow.

fungus garden

Leaf-cutter ants chew the leaves into a pulp, which they feed to the fungus.

Gardener ants take care of the fungus.

Waste, such as dead ants, is taken to the dump by waste handlers.

The fungus eats the leaves to grow.

Queen ants can lay up to 200 million eggs. These turn into maggotlike larvae.

Dumps can spread diseases.

Garbage dump

Waste is stored in special chambers. It is then carried out and dumped a safe distance away from the nest.

Larvae turn into hard pupae, which become ants.

Nurse ants take care of the eggs, larvae, and pupae.

Old food and dead ants can lead to disease.

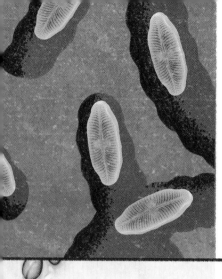

Single cells

Living things are made up of miniscule parts called cells. You contain trillions of them! However, most microbes are "single celled"—the whole creature is made of just one cell.

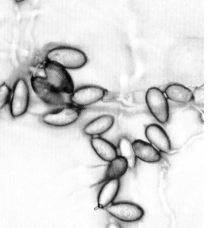

Troublemakers

Some soil microbes make plants sick. Raindrops can splash off soil, picking up and carrying these microbes to the leaves of plants above. Little plants on the ground can stop this from happening by catching the raindrops before they splash on the soil.

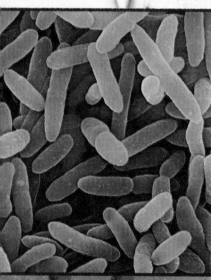

Hidden heroes

Microbes can do good things for plants. Some protect the roots of plants by releasing chemicals called antibiotics. These kill other microbes that can harm plants and improve the plant's ability to fight off disease. On top of that, some of them glow in the dark!

Soil spaces

Microbes help keep a good structure in soil. They create tunnels and caverns, and make a special glue that keeps the spaces open. Water and air, which plants need to stay alive, move through these spaces.

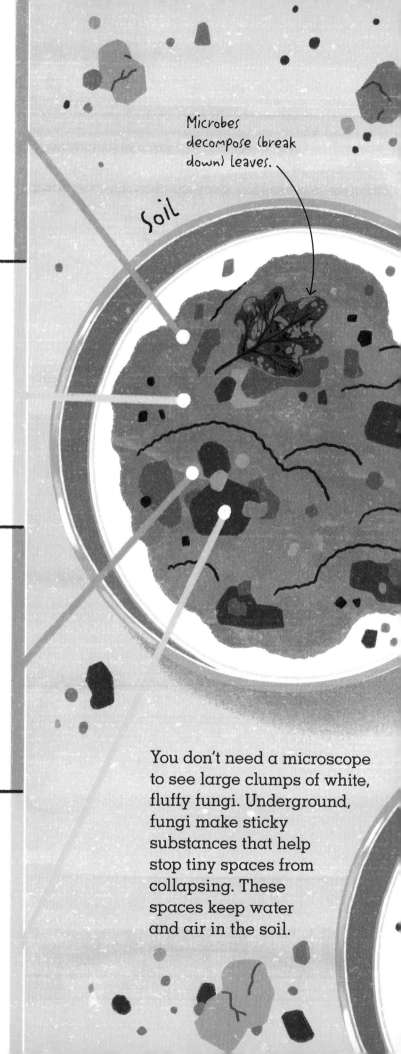

Microbes decompose (break down) leaves.

Soil

You don't need a microscope to see large clumps of white, fluffy fungi. Underground, fungi make sticky substances that help stop tiny spaces from collapsing. These spaces keep water and air in the soil.

TINY LIFE

A small amount of soil contains billions of tiny living creatures, called microbes. They can usually only be seen under a microscope, which is how scientists study them.

The trillions of microbes found in soil don't just sit around—they do a lot of useful jobs. For example, some change nutrients into forms that plants can absorb as food. This means that the plants can grow big enough for us to eat them ourselves!

A teaspoon of soil contains more microbes than there are humans on the Earth.

Algae

Fungi

Microbes can be seen in large numbers as blue and green slime on the surface of soil. These can be microscopic plants (algae), bacteria, or mixtures of both.

MICROBES IN ACTION

The world would be very different without microbes. From breaking down dead things to making oxygen for us to breathe, these pages show only a little of what they do.

Air maker

Humans need oxygen to breathe, but the air wouldn't be quite so full of it without bacteria! Some bacteria make this all-important gas.

Nostoc is a group of bacteria that makes oxygen.

Plant doctor

Some fungi, such as *Trichoderma citrinoviride*, live inside plants and make antibiotics (a type of medicine) for them to fight diseases.

Disease causer

Phytophthora infestans is a microbe that causes a disease in potatoes and tomatoes, called blight. It is responsible for many historic food shortages.

Many types of microbe can feast on one leaf.

Microbes break down animals as well as plants.

Eco-warrior

Methane is a greenhouse gas that causes global warming. *Methylocapsa gorgona* takes methane out of the air, because it needs the gas to survive.

Food Fixer

Some plants would find it tricky to survive without bacteria such as *rhizobia*. This type of microbe takes a gas called nitrogen from the air and uses it to make plant food.

Transformer

Fungi such as *Mortierella* break down dead plants and animals into new material. Other living things can then eat the broken-down material.

ALL THAT GLITTERS

If you dig a hole you'll probably hit a stone, and rubbing soil between your fingers will reveal a grainy texture. Rocks and minerals have been transformed into small bits in soil over thousands of years.

Rain freezes in cracks and expands to break off pieces of rock.

Rivers can transport stones away from where they formed.

Solid treasure

Stones can be rocks or minerals—the hard substances that rocks are made of. Rocks form in different ways. Some cool from lava spat out by volcanoes!

Dalmation stone

Rose quartz

Lapis lazuli

Marble

Rocks to pebbles

Rocks are crumbled and dissolved by rain and ice. This process is called weathering. The particles eventually become small enough to form part of soil.

Panning for stones

Precious stones are heavier than soil. They can be found by panning, or washing the soil off with water.

Sizing it up

Soil particles come in different sizes. Imagine a clay particle as a large coin. Next to it, silt would be as big as a tennis ball, and coarse sand the size of a hot-air balloon!

Clay particles look like tiny, flat plates.

Sand

Clay

Silt

Sand particles look like very small rock pieces.

Gold

Garnet

Citrine

Sandstone

The best soil for plants has not too much sand or clay.

Plant Food

Soil is made up of sand, silt, and clay particles. The amount of each affects how fertile soil is, how much water it holds, and how well water drains through it.

Both plants and animals can become fossils.

Fossils are the traces (such as footprints) or remains in rocks of living things from millions of years ago.

It can take eight years for soil as thick as card to form.

47

Carnivorous plants such as sundews and butterworts catch flies to eat with their sticky leaves.

Sundew

Marsh Labrador tea

Cranberry

Sphagnum moss

This plant is often used to make an herbal tea.

Common butterwort

Murumuru tree

Umbrella thorn tree

Laperrine's olive tree

Wetland soil

Peat soil in wetlands isn't just home to unique species of plants. It stores more carbon than any other type of soil. If this is released into the air as a gas, it traps heat and can speed up global warming.

Walking palm

Euphorbia echinus

There are more than 70,000 types of soil in the US alone.

Annona purpurea

Lobster claw

Lobster claw nectar is a favorite food of hummingbirds.

GROUND AROUND THE WORLD

A single country can contain thousands of soil types. Plants suited to each soil range from tall trees, which look like they have legs (the walking palm), to squat succulents.

Rain-forest soil

This is found in warm regions with plenty of rainfall. The soil has few nutrients, but millions of plant species are found there.

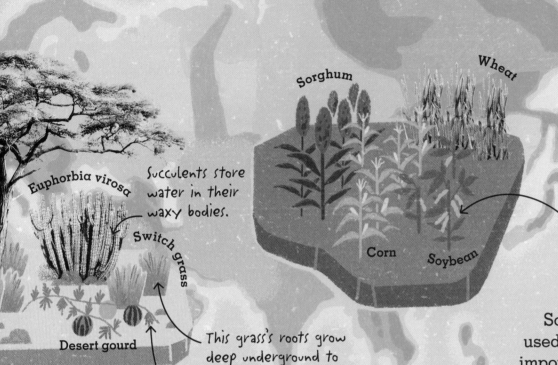

Sorghum

Wheat

Euphorbia virosa

Succulents store water in their waxy bodies.

Switch grass

Desert gourd

Corn

Soybean

Soybeans are used to make foods such as tofu.

This grass's roots grow deep underground to find water.

Drought-resistant herbs are important foods for desert animals.

Farmland soil

Soil with a lot of nutrients is used across the planet to grow important crops such as wheat. China is the world's biggest producer of food crops.

Dry-land soil

Dry soil is found in areas with low rainfall. Plants here have long roots and thick, fleshy stems to save water. The roots are important for holding the soil in place.

Plants can't grow in most of the frozen land of Antarctica.

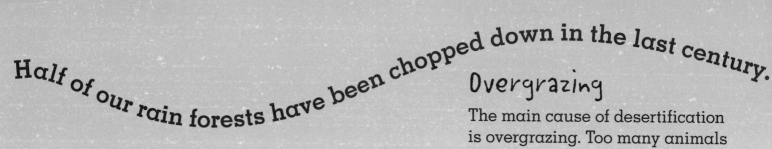

Overgrazing

The main cause of desertification is overgrazing. Too many animals grazing and trampling on plants can lead to the soil becoming bare. The wind then blows or the rain washes the bare soil away.

Deforestation

Trees are chopped down for fuel, to make things with, and to clear land for farming. If too many trees are cut down without new ones being planted, it leaves bare soil with no tree roots to hold the soil in place.

Wood is used to make paper.

Loose soil can be washed or blown away.

Only a few types of plants can grow in desertified land.

SOIL TO SAND

People's actions are causing healthy soil to lose its nutrients and turn into loose, dry sand. This process is called desertification. It is bad news for us and for the environment.

Dry land has few plants, which many animals need to feed on.

Overfarming

Too many crops take nutrients and water out of the soil. This means new plants are not able to survive in the soil.

Areas around today's deserts are most at risk of desertification.

Rain doesn't fall during a drought, which affects plants.

Global warming

A hotter planet could cause desertification in a lot of ways. For example, some crops don't grow as well in hotter weather. Less rainfall also leads to dry soil that blows away.

Desertified soil is too loose for plants to anchor their roots in well.

Over 100 countries are at risk of desertification.

Zai pits

Desertified land

Few things grow in sand. It also holds less carbon than fertile soil. If carbon is released into the air as a gas, it traps heat and can speed up global warming.

Tackling the problem

People are looking at ways of using desertified land. In some areas, plants can be grown in holes called zai pits. These collect water and can be filled with nutrient-rich animal poop or soil.

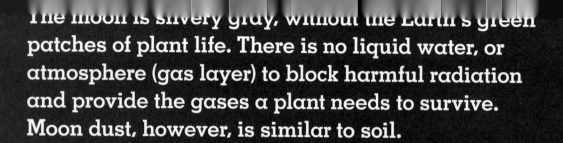

The moon is silvery gray, without the Earth's green patches of plant life. There is no liquid water, or atmosphere (gas layer) to block harmful radiation and provide the gases a plant needs to survive. Moon dust, however, is similar to soil.

Moon dust

There are no living things to create tiny tunnels and caverns in moon dust. On Earth, water, nutrients, and gases move through these spaces for plants to absorb.

Moon dust is mostly tiny bits of glass.

Craters are formed when large meteors hit the moon.

Moon rock forms from lava cooling on the surface.

True soil

Soil needs living things. These eventually form the organic matter inside it, as well as its structure. Even if you added water to moon dust, it would just form a paste.

The moon is constantly bombarded with meteors.

Explosive Formation

Moon dust is formed mainly by grinding and explosions, caused by meteors. The impact breaks the rocky surface into pieces.

Meteor impacts cause pieces of moon rocks to fly into space.

Studying lunar soil

People last went to the moon on the Apollo missions of the 1960s and 1970s. Astronauts collected moon dust to study back on Earth.

Astronauts drilled into the ground to collect samples.

Astronauts tried tasting moon dust!

Plants in lunar soil

Moon dust contains many of the nutrients in soil. Scientists have even been able to grow plants in soil that mimics moon dust. The plants grew for up to 50 days.

Tomato

Field mustard

Wheat

Cress

CAN PLANTS GROW ON MARS?

Humans may one day garden on Mars. The soil has the nutrients needed by plants, with toxins that could be removed. Mars, however, has no liquid water, so this would need to be produced for the plants. The plants would also need protection from harmful conditions.

Sort-of soil

Martian soil is very similar to moon dust. Neither contains living things to create spaces, which make soil suitable for plants.

The rover will drill down to look for microorganisms in the soil.

Martian rocks

Long ago it rained on Mars. The water froze in cracks on the rocky surface. The ice expanded and broke off tiny fragments of rock. These are still part of the soil today.

Mars's atmosphere is 95 percent carbon dioxide (a gas plants need).

The atmosphere

The layer of gas around a planet is called its atmosphere. Mars's thin atmosphere doesn't filter out harmful radiation from the sun, such as solar wind (particles that can damage anything they touch).

Investigating Mars

In 2022, The European Space Agency plans to send a rover to Mars. Its mission is to search for alien life that could be buried in the soil.

Plants have been grown in a copy of Martian soil.

Water on Mars

Mars's water has mostly been heated into a gas by the sun, and has floated off into space. Polar ice caps, however, remain.

The ice caps get so cold that gas freezes solid and falls from the air.

Astro-gardeners

To grow plants on Mars, a special greenhouse would be needed to protect the plants from the extreme temperatures. It would also stop them from exploding in the air, which has very low pressure.

Astronauts would grow vegetables.

A special greenhouse could add air pressure.

BE A SOIL SCIENTIST

Microbe meal

You will need: a trowel, card, a shovel, a pen, tape, a stick, and an old

Healthy soil is home to organisms, from earthworms to tiny microbes. If you've got a yard, bury a cotton sock to find out if the soil is full of hungry things. Make sure the sock is 100% cotton!

1. Dig a 7.9-in (20-cm) pit and put the soil on some paper.

2. Use a trowel to fill the sock with some of the soil.

3. Put the sock in the pit and cover it with the rest of the soil from the paper.

Worm hotel

You will need: a 2-liter disposable plastic bottle, scissors, garden compost,

Earthworms spend their lives hidden from view. Build them a worm hotel to discover what they do in the soil, before returning them to the soil to continue the good work.

1. Ask an adult to help you cut the bottle in half, being careful with the scissors. Add a 3.9-in (10-cm) layer of soil. Spray it with water.

2. Spraying water after each layer, add 0.2 in (0.5 cm) of sand, 0.2 in (0.5 cm) of compost, and 2 in (5 cm) of soil. Poke 0.5-in (1-cm) holes in the hotel with a pencil.

3. Dig in your yard or in a park to find five worms. Put them in the hotel. They'll burrow down, using the holes. Add leaves as food.

Perfectly wonky carrots

You will need: a patch of soil for growing, a trowel,

Stones and twigs are often removed from the soil before carrots are grown. This is so they grow straight down without objects blocking their way. See what happens otherwise...

1. Carrot seeds should be sown from April until July. Rake the soil to loosen it, and dig a 0.5-in (1-cm) deep row.

2. Sprinkle the carrot seeds along the row, about 10 for every 1 inch (2.5 cm) of length. Cover with soil.

Label the carrots with the date, your initials, and the plant name.

3. If there's no rain in the first few days, water the row and cover it with damp newspaper for a week or so.

100%-cotton sock.

4. Tape card to a stick to make a marker. Mark the spot.

5. Dig the sock up after eight weeks. If it's been eaten, with plenty of holes, the soil is healthy because it has a lot of organisms!

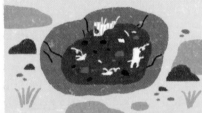

soil, sand, a pencil, a spray bottle, cardboard, leaves, and tape.

4. Worms like the dark! Wrap cardboard around the wormery to block out light. Spray the hotel with water daily.

5. After a week, see how the worms have changed the soil. There will be a lot of burrows, the layers will have begun to disappear, and the leaves may have been dragged into the soil.

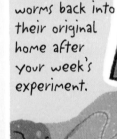

6. Release the worms back into their original home after your week's experiment.

a watering can, a rake, carrot seeds, newspaper, plant labels, and a store-bought carrot.

4. Water the carrots often but gently, at ground level.

5. When the plants are around 4-in (10-cm) tall, thin them to one plant every 2 in (6 cm) by pulling out the smaller ones.

6. After 16—20 weeks your carrots should be fully grown! Gently pull them out of the ground.

7. Compare the carrots to a store-bought one to see the difference!

TAKING CARE OF SOIL

To keep color-speckled insects and plenty of plants all around, we need to make sure we take care of the ground. We can do small things that have big effects.

Stay on the path

Plant roots hold soil in place so it doesn't get worn away by wind, rain, or feet. If the plants around a path are trampled and killed, it may get wider and wider as the soil disappears. In parks, make sure to stay on the path.

It takes about three to nine months to make compost.

Make compost

Fruit and vegetable waste breaks down into brown, crumbly compost. This can be mixed into the soil to help plants grow. Find out if special food-waste bins and collections exist in your neighborhood. If you have a yard, make your own compost pile!

Wildlife feeds on fungi growing on different types of wood.

Make tiny animal shelters

Find a shady spot in a park or your yard and make a pile of logs and twigs. Try to use as many different types of wood as possible. This makes an excellent shelter for beetles, centipedes, and spiders.

Leave soil alone

Digging disturbs soil animals. If you have a yard, choose an unused patch of it and let nature go wild! You can sprinkle native wildflower seeds here to help attract bees and butterflies. Ask permission first.

GLOSSARY

Bacteria
Type of microorganism

Burrow
Tunnel made by a creature, often to find food or for shelter

Carbon
Substance found in all living things and in the gas carbon dioxide

Carbon dioxide
Gas found in the air, also written as CO_2

Cast
Poop of a worm

Decomposition
Process of living things breaking down into their chemical building blocks after death

Deforestation
Process of the trees in a forest being cut or burned down

Desertification
Process of fertile soil becoming dry, loose sand

Ecosystem
Community of plants and animals in a single area

Fertile
Suitable for things to grow

Flower
Part of a flowering plant that makes seeds

Fungi
Group of living things separate from plants, animals, and bacteria

Gas
Substance, with no shape, that can be found in the air

Global warming
Process of the Earth becoming warmer

Insect
Small creature with six legs and a body with three parts

Invertebrate
Animal without a backbone

Larva
Newly hatched insect

Leaf
Part of a plant that turns nutrients, carbon dioxide, and oxygen into food for the plant

Microbe
Another name for a microorganism

Microorganism
Tiny living thing that can usually be seen only with a microscope

Mineral
Natural material that can be found in rocks

Network
Group of connected things, such as tunnels

Nutrient
Substance that a living thing uses to grow

Organic
Living or once living, and containing carbon

Organism
Living thing, such as a microbe, plant, or animal

Particle
Tiny piece of something

Pollutant
Substance that enters water or air and makes it unsafe

Predator
Animal that eats other animals

Prey
Animal eaten by another animal

Pupa
Early stage of life for some insects in which they grow a hard case and don't move around

Radiation
Particles or rays of energy that can be harmful

Root
Part of a plant that absorbs nutrients and water

Sediment
Bits that settle at the bottom of a body of water, such as a lake

Spore
Part of a fungus that could grow into a new fungus

Stem
Part of a plant that holds up the flowers and leaves

Topsoil
Top layer of soil, which contains a lot of organic matter

INDEx

ACKNOWLEDGMENTS

DK would like to thank: Katie Lawrence for editorial help; Katie Knutton, Ashok Kumar, Nimesh Agrawal, and Manpreet Kaur for design help; Polly Goodman for proofreading the book; Helen Peters for the index; and Cecilia Dahlsjö for her advice about ants. Many thanks to Rae Spencer-Jones and Simon Maughan at the RHS.